A Muddle & a Miracle

by Serena Fusek

Wider Perspectives Publishing   ∞ 2026 ∞   Newport News, Va.

The cover photography, poems and writings in this book are the creations and property of Serena Fusek: the author is responsible for them as such. Wider Perspectives Publishing reserves 1st run rights to this material in this form, all rights revert to author upon delivery. Author reserves all rights thereafter: Do not reproduce without permission except Fair use practices for approved promotion or educational purposes. Author may redistribute, whole or in part, at will, for example submission to anthologies or contests.

© 2026, Serena Fusek,
1st run complete in January 2026
Wider Perspectives Publishing, Hampton Roads, Va.
ISBN 978-1-964531-07-6

Contents

Echoes and Shadows
                    1

Kaleidoscope
                    28

I Dreamt I Dwellt
                    54

Moments
                    66

EKG Of A Stunned Heart
                    75

Echoes and Shadows

Dancing With Shadows

"Poetry is an echo
asking a shadow to dance."
~ Carl Sandburg

"Poetry is ghost language."
~ Tony Moffeit

1.

I've spent my life with echoes
dancing with the shadows
of ghosts.

The ghosts are me.
The ghost is mine

and I am the medium
that transcribes their messages
to the book.

2.

Poetry is the shadow on the wall
left behind when the dancer
whirled out of the light.

It is what remains
when everyone—even the host--
has gone home,
the book jumbled among
the empty glasses, dirty plates,
the wine stains.

Poetry is the salt
left on the napkin
where the tears dried.

3.

Poetry is whispers
from the moon,
dictation from the stars
transmissions from the galaxies
heard through the speakers
of an unplugged radio
at midnight.

Poetry is written in Enochian
no matter what language
is on the page.

Poetry is the shriek of madness
from the hidden family member
locked in the attic
or chained in the basement.
We don't hear her sobbing
we don't hear him screaming
but their voices
appear on the page.

Poetry is the voice
of the man without a tongue
singing.

Mindful

On the pond's bank
 sit still
as the egret. Let gnats
and mosquitoes swarm
until they grow bored. Let
your eyes become water
through which light passes
easily as fish.

Let the trees
bark and leaf
climb of ivy
tangle of honeysuckle
slide through your vision.
See the yellow flower,
spy the tiny orchid nestled
among the leaf mold.

Then the hawk materializes
on the branch. You find the deer child
hidden in the thicket. The raccoon
slips to water
washes its clever paws
as you watch and
the small brown sparrows
flitting through last year's brown leaves
lose their invisibility.

You see
the eyes   leaf green
hawk gold   soft as the doe's
watching you.

Memory of Queens

Dusk softens the summer day
when he rounds the curve
sees the three does
standing among the trees
each slim as a ballerina
with the high, slanted cheekbones
of a queen   shy eyes dark
as secrets.

One rounded ear flicks
the lead doe raises her head
and the three turn
dissolve into green dark
like women of the Fae
who appear but
are not there.

The Next Breath

Out of invisibility
the crow's cry
ratchets down dawn
fades
into the hush
of fog. As if
from far away
water sighs
along unseen banks.
No breeze moves
among clotted wisps of air.
The world--
caught between tock and tick--
balances
on the stillness
of a dandelion puff
waiting for the next breath
to fly.

Breath and Silence

The breath of the first word "Light"
sped through the universe

a wind that blew open
the gates of darkness.

Write these words in ink
distilled from darkness.

Under stones, in cellars
in the vault of my ribs
darkness is deaf.

It turns its bad ear
to the wind.

In the tomb darkness hears
only silence

that existed
before words were dreamed.

Love, the light of the world
reveals itself in the dark.

Angels sing light. The angel of darkness
was the brightest angel of the host.

Darkness let us descend
into the silence of caves
where the fish have no eyes
and bats see with their ears.

Wind

"...I think of my father's whistle,
    ways it called the sundered shadows
    of a family into the house"
    ~ Dave Smith

My father's whistle--
shrilled around two
fingers to ascend
Route 28"s traffic din
and snare our ears
two backyards away--
does not echo down
the years. It's gone
with the body that
blew, with the house
he whistled us
home to.
What remains is
the air that passed
through his lungs.

Yoga: Just Breathe

Breathe in.
Breathe out.

Exhale
the warmth in my lungs
the pain in my hip
the beat of my heart,
its red fire.

Inhale
   the air exhaled
by wolf   by egret
by the friend I've yet to meet
by the woman on the mat
beside me.

Exhale:
   my life
leaks into the world

returns
on the inhalation
rich with spices and perfume
of the sun's heat
the wind's spirit
the breath from the tiny lungs
of the singing bird.

From me
to the deer the ant
the mother in Afghanistan
the child soldier in Africa

back to me
from the mouse
in the cupboard
the raccoon raiding the feeder
the lovers across town.

This air
my father whistled
a lifetime ago
to call me home.

Silence Hears

Silence hears everything.
Silently the deer browse on roadsides.
Night fills their eyes.

Night turns. Stars circle the sky.
What coming conjunction
calls the spirits back to earth?

The deer stand at the gate
that passes through them.
These ancient trees
don't grow in our woods.

The music in their hearts
beats through the dark.
Night fills their eyes.

I search the night
for the whisper of his pulse.
Silently the deer browse.

What coming conjunction
calls the spirits back?

The eyes of the deer swallow the night.
Silence hears everything.
Silently they watch me pass.

A Muddle & a Miracle

A rift twists the darkness.
He followed the deer
into the greenwood.

Silence hears everything.
Night fills their eyes
The dark seals my mouth
but I cry his name.

Scraps From Funeral Dresses

As I drive under a sky
drenched in blue an
old tune rocks the radio
and I'm suddenly seventeen
in love with eyes blue
as this sky until

I glide through a curve
into the slammed door memory
of closed eyes in a coffin

and my bones rattle:
bones in which my dead
rise to be tallied.
Under this blue that veils
endless night I name each--
Mother, Father, Great Aunt Ethel
the boy with music in
his crippled body the man
whose blue gaze never met mine
though he taught me to see--
a rosary strung with drops
of blood.

Children fill their space
above the earth but
my flesh   nerves marrow
that knew their touch
aches from their absence
like pain that flares in scars

when thunderheads mass.
I drive under shining sky
but in the corner of my eyes
tatters of darkness flap
like scraps from funeral dresses.

Armageddon

In the end God
steps from time's river
returns to eternity.
Yet eternity does not last.
Bored on that dry shore
without His tricksters, his clowns
his troubled and troubling children
who, calling His name
call Him into being,
He makes again
what He destroyed.

The Book of Revelations
is not prophecy
but history. He cleansed
our memory
but specters of
fire, of plague,
of a white horse--
stained red to its withers--
picking its way through
agony-torqued corpses
torment prophets
as abused children
forgetting the wound
remember a dream
a nightmare,
a vision of screams.

Past is Present: a Circle Dance

You were a king,
I your favorite wife.
After sixty years
I died
before the mourners
at your funeral
could return home.

We had one summer
as the grapes
grew fat and sweet.
The air hung fragrant
with russet and wine
when you returned
to the war. The rest
of my life was lived
around the hole
of your death.

I taught you
the Charleston.
You taught me
to drive. We already knew
how to love each other.
We've done it
through so many lives.

We have not met
but your presence
shades my life
like a great tree.
I examine the globe
whisper the names
of places you might be:

Sri Lanka, Mumbai,
Vienna, Venice.
Perhaps you're in Rio
composing a samba,
driving a truck
across Siberia
or strolling around
this corner where--
caught by the changing traffic light--
I wait.

Origami

Take paper
made from tree   from reed.
Fold   open
fold again
the paper flowers.

In your heart hold the wish
for health   long life
fold the crane--
one of a thousand--
wrapping the paper
around the prayer
hiding it inside the crease.

Hands crimp   fingers press
a square of paper.
Restless fiddling
three dimension doodling
suddenly reveals
a unicorn.

In the park we watched
the swans — Zen masters — float
serenely among the clouds
reflected in the pond.
Your hands played with
a piece of pearly paper

turning a corner under
bringing a flap over
smoothing edges --
capturing inside each furrow
the second   quarter second
it was made.

Pinch   pleat   pocket into
pocket   a maze in which
time ceased to flow:
the moment you kissed me
sun sparkling tears in my eyes
tucked inside
this paper swan.

The Monkey's Paw

> "We began as mineral.
> We emerged into plant life
> and into the animal state,
> then to being human....
> ....And always we have
> forgotten our former states."
> ~ Rumi (translated by
> Coleman Barks)

Through her human skin
other selves well up
like a spring gushing
from the rock
of her bones--
amoeba
fish frog
the first reptile
tiny as a skink;
inside her hand
the monkey flexes its paw.

In the nucleus
of her cells
she is the fox
slinking through the garden.
She is the rabbit
battling crows that
threaten her young.
She is the crow
returning to the cries
and gaping beaks in
her nest.

Serena Fusek

She is the tree
sheltering the nest.

Fin claw
paw—one extra or
one less bit
on the helix twist
might become
four separate fingers
an opposable thumb
and the cat lounging in her lap
could sit upright
and knit.

In Our Place

We are made of
ghosts and angels.
We are by-products
of star formation.
The mathematics
of infinity
plot the patterns
of our forms.
Maps of
solar systems
are implanted
in our cells.

Some of our angels
have forgotten the way
to Heaven,
some of our ghosts
encoded their torment
into our genes.
We crawl across
a blue rock
on the far edge
of the cosmos
lift our heads
into darkness
and star fire.

Handy

Hand and brain
evolved together.
Hand grew nimble
brain grew larger
and invented tools.

The brain instructs.
The hand grasps the tool
tightens the bolt,
carves the wood block
into a toy horse,
pounds the nail
that builds the house.

The ballpoint skates
across the page
guided by small movements
of the wrist where
the pulse jumps.
It draws
the loops the swirls
curls into the words
of the poem

celebrating the hand.

From secret mazes
of the mind
hand makes
the world.

Watched
(Living on the Street)

Even the air
       has eyes   they look
           they watch   I shamble
down the sidewalk
    the eyes
        crawl
            over my skin like
                bees
                    licking my sweat
    the grime of the street
and they sting
            a prick
    a shock
            bright as a silver pin

    and the sky
the sky is the worst
              one blue stare
      inflaming my sight
                      its cobalt rays
    penetrating my bones.

In the girders of the El
    the pigeon has its nest,
by the fast food dumpster
    the stray cat has its den
        but I have
    no address
        no wall

Serena Fusek

at my back
> no door
>> to slam against
> the glares   the gapes
>> to shut out the
> molesting gawks
touching
> scratching
>> clutching
> at my skin
trying to get in.

Homed people
who can retreat behind walls
> close curtains
>> stroll this August day
> in shorts and tees
>> legs
>>> exposed.
I
hide
> in my long coat
buttoned to my chin
>> pull my cap
> low
>> shuffled along   my gaze
>>> on the ground
and their eyes
> sting.

2

Kaleidoscope

The Future is a Kaleidoscope of Dimensions Turning Through Colorful Possibilities

The tube brass
the tube cardboard
a toy that you turn to see
shifting colors
changing patterns
changing possibilities.

Bits of glass
chips of glitter
tumble through

a shifting mosaic
that slips   slides
 blooms and dies

dimensions folding into dimensions

then unfolding

circling until
the original arrangement returns--
like the night sky
traveling   through the seasons
always returning
to the Hunter and his sword.

Designs change
at the twist of a wrist
like shuffling Tarot cards--
all those futures
rippling into possibility
then vanishing
without being glimpsed
at the deck's next riffling--
the Lady, the Seeker, children
in the sun, monsters crawling
out of a moon lit well..

It's all done
with mirrors
like a magician's trick--
will he pull
from the tall, tubular hat
a white rabbit
or a rattlesnake?

All the Reasons

Why?

Because the world is round
but my heart is a closed fist.

Because you are a dream
elusive as a fox--
a flash of auburn
vanishing into the brambles.

Because my heart is a fist
with scarred knuckles.

Because my fist trembles.

Because the bus is coming
and I want to miss it.

Because you put your child
on the school bus
and don't know if
you'll get them back.

Because the rain is always followed
by the sun.

Because if there is no rain
the earth cracks
and so do our lips.

Because I never wanted
to be nice. I wanted to be
interesting.

Because the world is a what
and a why and where
is God and do the stars
really sing?

(What do they sing?)

Because questions
are the world's glory
(same verse)

and mystery is true name
of God.

Because my favorite word is joy
but a crow peers through my eyes
and his shriek echoes through my skull.

Because the blind angel
watches the spot where
my grave will be...

Because my heart is a fist
with scarred knuckles
that ache in the rain.

Because the marsh is empty
and the sun lies on the water
like a steel door.

Because my heart is a fist
with knuckles that bleed
through the scars.

Because the world
is a muddle
and a miracle.

Because we humans are
flawed creatures but
dogs love us.

Because the word mystery
with all its 'y's'
has the question
lurking inside it.

Because it is raining
and my knuckles ache.

City Sinking

Under the waves
that scrabble and claw
at the city's walls,
under the waves
that—in the glow
of the ancient sun--
gleam like tarnished diamonds,
glitter like glass
gone radioactive
at a frequency
almost audible--

under the waves
into which the city sinks
like a woman
sleepy with opium
sliding under
the scummy bubbles
of her bath

waves that swallow
cellars, ballrooms,
infamous bedrooms:

no need to imagine
what lies submerged
under waves
sluggish with sludge
steeped in a millennium's muck

every high tide
laps above
the penultimate stain
fouling the stones.
Soon what skulks
under the waves
will slither through
city streets.

Rubble

The world is full of ruins
ancient cities buried under new cities--
they say there are seven layers of Troy--
Roman mosaics discovered
under modern Italian street works.

Broken walls the only remains
of ancient cathedrals.

Towns swept away in storms
blasted to shards in wars
buried under volcanic ash
swallowed by rain forest
or desert.

Futures ended, fenced off,
the tree growing in the mud
on the factory floor.

And Hiroshima
rebuilt over ash and shadows
haunted by the isotopes

that brood in silos

hoping to make new ruins
because ruins
are the natural order of the world.

That gleaming tower just built?
Dust, weather, time
already erodes its shine.

We live in ruins
and pretend our roofs
will always stand.

The Broken Grave

In the abandoned
weed choked cemetery
the roots of the maple tree
spread rampantly until

they break
into her grave.
They split her cheap pine box
slide over
under and around
her bones. A century
without touch
now the roots embrace her.

They sip her skeleton's calcium
lap up their phosphorus
lick the DNA from her dried marrow.

She becomes
bark   wood   golden sap
that rises through the trunk
spreads into the branches
seeps into the sweet smelling leaves

gives her back
the sun.

Painting Gershwin's Rhapsody in Blue

From the bell of the horn
in the picture's corner
that wail of
blue

a clarion
color pure and shining
as brushed steel
tempered with gold
rises

out of city canyons
riding the wings
of pigeons
and aeroplanes
skimming the gray walls
of skyscrapers

the long azure swoop
only a little darker than sky
sweeps up the canvas
climbing toward clouds.

Near the top--
almost into heaven--
it curves back.

Drops of green
red, gold
drift
down the sky--

fireworks
exploding into
orchestra.

The Beloved of Whom the Poet Speaks

This is a song
whispered at midnight

as the candles on the piano
sputter toward darkness

for the Beloved
of whom the poet speaks.

The Beloved
who cannot be named
who has many names

whose likeness
is a crayon sketch
seen through a steamed up window.

The Beloved
who may not see me

who is the source
of all magic

whose voice is silence

that stings me
to song and verse

praising
the Beloved's arrival

which may never happen.

It Isn't, It Is

It isn't an angel
it's a raven.

It isn't prophecy
it's regret.

That isn't someone
knocking on the door—
it's the ghost in the wind
rattling the lock.

It isn't a flower.
It's a silk rose.
The bee turns away.

This pillow isn't comforting.
It's hard as a heart.

That's not the sunrise.
Something burns in the night.

It isn't coffee in the cup.
It's whiskey.
It's hemlock.

It isn't exactly the truth.
It isn't exactly a lie.
It's a story sifting the clues.

It isn't a dress.
It isn't a suit.
It's a shroud.

It isn't an angel.
It's a raven
 a single raven

sorrow
    riding
        on
            its wings.

"It's a Bird..."

There was a bird--
it was an owl
it was a crow
it was a hummingbird
among the roses.
It was a day dream--
it wasn't a bird
but a butterfly--
a soul returned
to this earth where butterflies
mingle with hummingbirds
among the roses.

It wasn't an angel
but it might have been
an eagle
soaring over the creek
by the secret military base.
It wasn't an eagle--
it was a drone
watching—like God—
from the sky.

It was a bird:
a small yellow bird
cut from cardboard
mounted in a small box
with a paper butterfly.
It can be seen
not in the park
but in the museum.

                        (for Joseph Cornell)

Fun House

Where am I?
 Here
   no, there--

   it's all a mirage
     in a house of mirrors

my reflection
  reflected
     and that reflection
thrown back
  tossed forward
like a ball
  I cannot catch.

I stand here--
   but I'm over there
my feet are grounded
on this floor
My self is grounded
in this body
   that is here
      or over
         there.

There are two of me
      there are three of me--
  now four.
One is my ghost
   ectoplasm fades from the glass
      like the mist of breath.
One is someone
     I could have been
One is someone
    I might have been
       in another life--
and one is me
   I guess.

Mirror Mirror
who is most fair--
   the me trying to laugh
at the distortions
    the me disappearing
or the me
      screaming
like a rabbit
  with its leg in a trap
somewhere
     over there?

What Happens in the Mirror

"the spin of something, inside the/mirror".
~ Tony Moffeit

There is a swirl of motion
in the mirror
reflection of the front door opening
a spin of night and stars
of night and snow
of frost that melts from the glass
as someone enters,
a shadow clouding the silver.

The door never moved
is latched and locked
remained solidly closed.
Someone came in.
Or someone did not come in.
A flash passed through the mirror
a shadow passed across the mirror.
No one was in the room
but there was movement
a churn of winter chill...

Your presence in my life
is a shadow passing
through the mirror
a glimmer in the glass
a quick fog of breath
drawn somewhere else,

  a spiral of light   gone.

More Visible By Guess

In the mirror's flat sheen
my face floats
eyes peering
into eyes.

In the thin glass
the room behind
is duplicated

like a still photo

until something
like a ripple
shivers across the surface
and down my spine.

Something hides
deep in the mirror
where the little fishes
glint like stray pieces of moon
something lurks
down in the mud
where the lilies root

something ancient
before earth dreamed
the softness of mammals
something that oozes
its huge bulk--

something more visible
by guess
than glance –

through the murk.

Eddies of its passing
flicker inside the glass

surge through my veins.

In the mirror's flat sheen
my face floats
pale as the moon.

Of the Roses, Only Thorns

Nothing remains
but the poem
and the cold sun
rising each morning
to shine on
frost blackened rags
of the garden.
Of the roses remain
only thorns,
the petals lost
in the poem
that is closed in the book.

Afterwards

Afterwards--
it was all afterwards.

The sky blanched
all color blanking out.
Voices, laughter, the hum of living
erupted in the screech of static.
The air froze
until it seared like flame.

Afterwards
the sky blinked blue again.
Afterwards
a bird warbled a cheerful aria
that trembled along tattered nerves.
Afterwards
the cold...

Afterwards
the sky might be blue
or streaked with storm,
the bird might sing
or shriek.
It was all the same.

Afterwards
was snow falling
gray as ash.

It was all afterwards.

3

I Dreamt

I Dwellt

I've Been Lost Here Before

"I think I've been lost here before."
~ overheard conversation

I think I've been lost here before.
Where is here? This place where
I am instead of where
I'm suppose to be. This place
that keeps pulling me back
that distorts and twists
the road like a badly tied ribbon
and I make the same wrong turn
return
to this wide place in the road
this place of heat and loneliness...

Or is it that my destination
doesn't want me
pushes me away whenever I near

and these second growth saplings
this mosquito-breeding puddle
this sudden cardinal song
breaking the stillness
tries to offer
refuge?

A Quiet Voice

The eagle soars
against a background
of fir trees and gem-blue sky,
circles the river
that rushes around glacial boulders

stretches one claw
casually plucks out a trout

and with long sweeps of its wings
gracefully as a dancer
turns
and climbs

up the TV screen.

A quiet voice
with diction flinty
as river rocks
informs us

"The mother eagle
hunts for food
to feed her chicks."

Of course she hunts for food.
What else would she feed her chicks?
Poetry?

Eagles don't need poetry.
They have the air.

The Kind of Light

> "the kind of light cafe winds shake
> from parasols"
> ~ Gary Kissick

a swipe of lilac
    swept with a line
        of lemon-silver

              a shine
of white

    spark of lime
of azure

a tremble
      of pink
    shiver of rose
          flickering into
    papaya   mango

blink

swipe of lime
    swept with a line
        of lavender---

the kind of light
    cafe winds
        shake
into a poem

I Dreamt I Dwelt
in Marble Halls

The walls were cold
even in summer.
Winters were arctic.
You can't hang pictures
from marble walls
you can't keep rugs
from skidding
across marble floors.
The slightest sound echoes
echoes
echoes....
The bed may be satin
but lovemaking
becomes everyone's entertainment.

Walking marble floors
can be dangerous
unless you wear rubber soles
(no hand tooled, high heeled
leather boots). To descend
or ascend
the stairs you must cling
to the banister--
which looked like gold
but was (more likely) brass--
until your hand cramps.

But when I took off my shoes
in my soft socks
I could slide across the floors
like a skater on ice.
Whee…!

He Departed Before He Arrived

He departed
before he arrived--
changed his mind
before he reached the town line
turned away

turned into a crow
who fell in love
with the sky
(who can blame him?)

turned into a dark angel
who glimmers through my dreams.

I look to the west
hope to spy him coming back
a black figure against brilliant horizon
but all I see
are approaching clouds
soaked with rain
thick with snow.

Each day
I put out peanuts
for the crows.

My Story

I roamed the world around
and unlike Amelia Earhart
I returned home
to my little cottage
behind the fence
where the gates
have rusted open.

I went out
and the whole world took me in.
I traveled by plane   by ship
rode motorcycles
and one summer drove
a little red Corvette
that tore across the desert
like a zipper down
the back of a dress.

The dust of a thousand roads
settled in my lungs
as I limped home
through the open gate
that always let me
come back.

Airplane seats
motorcycle saddles
the low slung bucket seat
from which I guided the Corvette —

now I settle into
this desk chair
take my next journey
along these roads
of memory.

Night Heavy With Stars

Stars wild
as the foxes
that run across the hills.
Stars that hang
across the heavens
as autumn's apples
hang from the trees.

Stars that light the way
as she and the little dog
go for the day's last walk.
Stars that pulse
like their two hearts.

The fragrance of apples
sweetens the crisp night.
They meander at the dog's pace
as she names the apples--
Rome, Honey Crisp, Jonagold
and the stars--
Betelgeuse, Arcturus
Rigel, Polaris.
The Milky Way spills
 down the sky
like cider from the press.

In the core of each apple
a star--
cut it across the middle and see.
In each beating heart
the dust of a star
flows like light.

In the orchard
foxes settle
beneath the trees.
The girl   the little dog
turn their heads
toward bed.

Stars run across the hills.

Lock Down 2020

A new morning. I wake
to a world I don't know.
There is my chair,
bowl, tea kettle
and the cat wants breakfast
as she does each day
no matter what the news is.

Milk is getting low--
where find more?

Outside the silence
of cars that remain
in their driveways.
All doors are closed
tightly as enemy gates.
The newspaper
has not been delivered

and the mother
strolling past
my driveway is not
the young woman
and her small daughter
from next door

but a mountain lion
and her two cubs.

Moments

Night on Skyline Drive

Blake said angels
at night passed
through fields where
by day lambs had nibbled
and the song says
Spirit is moving
all over the land.

On Skyline Drive
starlight walks the ridges
and the moon whispers
down the white line
of road wrapped around
mountain curves

the owl's call
falls down the tremolos of air
and the dark breathes
through the lungs
of the deer.

Night Passes

The night passes
on the paws
of the wolves
who prowl
across lawns
around corners
of houses,
beneath the sleeper's window —
ghosts of smoke
and the ashes of roses.

Inside Their Veils

Rain fell
through the April night.
On the maple
on the red buds
the tender new leaves
reached out
like the hands of children,
cradled each raindrop.

In the dark
the trees shimmered
inside their veils
of rain.

Breathe Into the Dark

In the soft night
daffodils and cherry blossoms
breathe into the dark.
Tender leaves uncurl
like baby fists.

Under the handicap ramp
the stray cat nurses
five just born kittens.

Someone asleep
suddenly opens her eyes
to endless starlight

The Stars, a Bright Host

The stars —
a bright host —
crowd the sky.
Among them
the new moon passes
invisible
as a doe
stepping between
sleeping houses.

Down the street
a dog suddenly
barks. In the garden
of her flowered sheets
a woman turns over,
hears a voice
she once loved.

As the World Woke

As the world woke
as the trees stretched into buds
the sky opened its blue eye
and the birds began
their loving clamor

he stepped into
silence.

Serena Fusek

Moments

1.

Drinking tea....
      steam carries the
           fragrance of peach
into the room.
Autumn afternoon shadows
fall across the kitchen floor
but summer sunshine
floods my mouth.

2.

A cup
of chamomile tea
the moon through
the window
listening to the night
breathe.

Not Even the Tip of a Tail

You were a dream
elusive as a fox —
a flash of auburn
vanishing into the brambles

not even the tip
of a tail
waving goodbye.

You were
a white deer
ghosting
through dawn's mist

gone
in the glare
of sunrise.

Serena Fusek

5

EKG of a

Stunned Heart

EKG of a Stunned Heart

Static
jitters through the brain
the sizzle of lightning

a storm of white fires
spikes and troughs
like the EKG
of a stunned heart

stings the air
with sparks
that prick like thorns

and through it the glimpse
the flash
of the angel.

The hard, ascetic
beautiful face
eyes blue
as heaven's confining walls

wavers into
and out of focus

vanishes in a burst
of temporary blindness

reappears
pale as a dream
fading into day…

She staggers.
The angel standing vigil
over the grave's empty bones
solidifies into stone
the pitted face
with its unseeing eyes
tilts toward the tree tops

while a nimbus of wings
sweeps the sky.

Invocation to the Angels

Angel of vengeance
give me your wrath.

Angel of waste places
scour me clean
as Sahara sands.

Angel of fire
fill me with your fury.

Angel of fury
wrap me in your fire.

Angel of revelation
the streets burn.
Who will quench
the flames?
Will anyone plant flowers
in the ashes?

Angel of tribulation
you live as close to me
as my skin and breath.

Angel of storms
I whistle you down
fill me with your power
tear up the flowers
smash life's tree.

Serena Fusek

Angel of silence
teach me to scream
so loud so high
that the world
cracks like a crystal glass.

Angel of death
I spit in your eye-
less sockets.

Angel of Armageddon
your four horsemen ride
through my bones
along the road of my nerves
and I am become death

because the Angel of joy
the Angel of light
left the land
in darkness lit
by incendiary bullets
by the hidden fires
of refugees   low watt lamps
behind black-out curtains.

Angel of Sanctuary
why have you locked your doors?

Angel of the cemetery gates
shelter me behind your iron bars
where stone angels
with sightless eyes
will wrap their wings
around me.

A Darkness So Massive

And the Angel
was a darkness so massive
that from horizon to horizon
it blotted out the heavens.
In its skirts
lightning seethed and crackled
and the bones of the people
shone like x-rays through their flesh.
Like the dragon
it roared and screamed
songs of its glory
until the air
could carry the sound no more
and cracked into silence.
The people fell into the dirt
blood trickling from their ears.
It strode across the land
searing the earth.
Fires followed like puppies.

When it had passed
the people sat
among the rubble
scratching the static
that still festered
beneath their skin
and looked to heaven

from whence—says the Psalm--
comes help.
The sky
bled of all blue
remained empty.

The Angel of Wrath

walks to and fro
through the world
crowned with a shattered halo
and wherever it passes
the people seethe
with anger that flares
up their bones
like a fire in a midden heap
sears their brains.
Clutch the cudgel
grip the gun--
someone is the enemy
someone believes
the wrong beliefs
someone doesn't trust angels.

Someone needs to die
for the crime
of being alive.

Quartet

Four angels
four horsemen
on steeds of lightning
steeds of radioactive fire
ride up and down
the world.
For millennia the names
of Michael of Gabriel
tethered them
but by the prophecy
their bonds are slashed.
Fired by the Lord's anger
they whip their steeds
until bloody spittle
flies around the iron bits.
The world trembles
with the pounding of hooves.

The Angel of Armageddon
in seared fingers
holds their broken leashes
and the sun collapses
through the event horizon.

There is No Angel of Music

Angels are music.

God didn't speak the first word,
 he sang it (in B flat).
And the stars appeared
 and the angels.

 The stars still hum that first note.
 Angels, however,
became entire choirs
complete symphonies.

As carbon life forms are held together by electrical current,
 angels are held together by song.

The big steel ears
hear the B flat
hum of the stars.

Stars are radioactive.
Are angels?
Is radiation a form of music?

The Webb Telescope, they say
will be able to see back to very beginning
but will it hear that first note
that trumpet blast
that exhale that woke
possibility and made it
real?

Will the Webb find heaven?
Is it out there anywhere?

Or is our idea of heaven the piece of song inside us?

Van Gogh painted Starry Night
in which the stars are presences
mad as a roil of angels.
He also cut off his ear.

Because, maybe, humans
should not hear angel song.

Where He So Intently Stares

In the painting
the saint--
his eyes wide
with fear
or ecstasy--
raises his gaze
to the sky
focusing on the blue
that will yield angels,
wheels of light,
or the face of God
that will destroy him.

When we look
to where he
so intently stares
when we raise our eyes
above the trees
and cathedral spires
we see only
vultures.

The Cathedral Fell

The cathedral fell
into ruin   destroyed
by war or fire or
loss of faith.

The roof caved in
allowing the night sky
with all its heavy stars
to press down
on the abandoned saints.

Moonlight flickers
where candles burned.

Freeze and heat
gale-lashed storms
cracked the windows.
Like jewels scattered from a king's hand
bits of stained glass
speckle the stone floor.
The splintered edge of St. Francis's robe
shard of an angel's wing
tears at the wind

that sings through the nave
filling the silence
from the ruined choir.

On a pile of leaves
blown into a corner
three wolf cubs
sleep against
their mother's warm side.

In what's left of the rafters
three crows roost.

It is God's favorite church.

Scripture

In the abandoned church--
the congregation dwindled
the preacher died--
the mice chew up the Bibles
to make nests.
"In the Beginning":
a litter of mice is born
among the pages of Genesis.

Serena Fusek

The Wild God

This is God who loves the ruined churches
where the animals settle—mice in
the wainscoting   wrens and sparrows
nesting in the rafters
where the roof fell away.
The statue of Mary shelters
a litter of raccoons behind
her skirts.

The altar
 the gold
the glitter of the windows
the pews
all removed.
 A tree grows
where the altar stood.

Because this God isn't
a stuffy old man
who wants robes and gold crosses
wine, bread, the bowed backs
of people who won't raise
their faces to His sky.
 He doesn't need the drone
of badly sung hymns
 when He can hear wren song
 wolf howl.

The Wild God
is the God of the Book
that is written in
in fur, in feathers
in the leaves
of the trees
in our blood.

The Book of the Wild God

This God wrote His first letters
in the words that grow the tree.
It is printed
in each leaf that
litters the stone floor
of the ruined church

in the blood and bone
of the raccoon kits
sheltered behind Mary's skirts

in the feathers of the wren.

These words need no scribe
to write them on dry and brittle paper,
they need no flawed translation.
Each word is perfectly expressed.
The wren sings their notes
every morning.

We have no need to memorize
Bible verses. Each
of us perfectly expresses
the passages of
His true Book.

Secretary to the Stars

Every night she took dictation
from the stars.
She sat at a little table
by the window
pen poised
over the notebook
letting their voices
guide her hand.

The stars spoke through
the hollows in her bones
like whispers through reeds
and her hand responded
started writing
before the words reached
her hearing.
She understood nothing
the voices said
but her hand wrote
something
someone could read.

The stars were the first,
 created before even the angels.
They have seen the face of God--
that vision is the radioactive fire
at their cores.

The stars watched
God seize the darkness
twist it into creation.

The stars should communicate
with a scientist.
They should send their pronouncements
to a prophet.

Instead they spoke
to this unknown woman
who wrote their messages
in a notebook
she put into a drawer
never read..

It is the Angel

Every evening
when she leaves work
she cuts through the cemetery
clumping along paths
between the graves
on aching feet.
In her thrift shop black coat
she looks like a mourner
but she ignores all the graves.

It is the angel
she comes to visit--

In its decades long vigil
over a grave empty
of all but brittle bones
the angel has been battered
by sun rain and chill
that blunts all grace
carved into its stone

blurs the face

to pitted eyes
staring blindly
at a heaven
that cannot be reached.

She knows that yearning.
She lays her hand
on a cold wing
that will never open

trudges on.

The Center Does Not Hold

Rain streams
from the swollen sky

drags the last leaves
into the street

where their colors dim
go out. Down the wet road

veiled by the torrent
someone wrapped

in darkness
(a black coat or

black wings) appears
or maybe a hole

opens in the day
where the center

has collapsed. All warmth
seeps into gray

drains down the sewers
with the gurgle
of autumn's rain.

Trail to the River

1.

The trail through the grass
leads down to the river.
Nobody drowned--
this is the path
snow melt followed.
Someone in a dark coat
trudges toward the bridge.
The sky is gray,
a nasty wind nips.
Nobody drowned--
the path
was made by snow melt.

2.

The grass bows
under a low
sneaky wind
that almost erases
the path.
Sky and river
are gray.
Someone in a coat
like a shroud
shambles toward
the bridge.
Nobody drowned.
Why am I so chilled?

3.

The chill
in the wind
blows off the river
that still holds winter
in the black mud
at its depths.
The trail
was made by
snow melt
or muskrat.
The coat
bent nearly in half
crosses the bridge.

Nobody drowned.
The bones
of the child
nobody missed
lie under the bridge
above high water.

Angel of Lost Bones

Angel of those who die
and their bones are never found.
Bones bleaching on a hillside
crumbling in an abandoned house.
The old man who died alone
and none were left to miss him
because he was the last.
The bones of a woman buried
in an unmarked grave
by her murderer. The bones of those
searched for but never found.
Bones cleaned by vultures and ravens--
the angel's emissaries.
Bones buried in the lava of Pompeii
burned in the firestorm of Dresden.
Shards of unidentified bones
left in the crematoriums of the camps.
Bones buried without a name
in a potter's grave.

Every femur rib splinter
every scrap of calcium dust and DNA
the angel knows   holds
sacred.

When the name on your stone fades
this angel will claim your bones.

Spirit Moves

Spirit moves through the night
silently on the owl's wing
in the luminous eyes of the deer
in the fur of the rabbit.
The grass knows the thought
of its footsteps
tree leaves stir without movement
in its breath.
It passes the window of children
dreaming in their deepest sleep
and the child who dies of fever
is taken in Spirit's arms
and lifted to God.
It moves through the breath
of roosting birds a touch soft
as feathers.
The possum raises a near-sighted gaze
a pink nose that smells nothing
but knows richness sweet
as a fallen peach.
The flowers mingle their fragrances
the song of their colors
into its essence.
And as we lie in our beds
or read by the window
Spirit surrounds us
with grace.

Indexed

Dancing With Shadows	2
Mindful	4
Memory of Queens	6
The Next Breath	7
Breath and Silence	8
Wind	10
Yoga: Just Breathe	11
Silence Hears	13
Scraps From Funeral Dresses	15
Armageddon	17
Past Is Present: A Circle Dance	18
Origami	20
The Monkey's Paw	22
In Our Place	24
Handy	25
Watched	26
The Future is a Kaleidoscope of Dimensions Turning Through Colorful Possibilities	29
All the Reasons	31
City Sinking	34
Rubble	36
The Broken Grave	38
Painting Gershwin's Rhapsody in Blue	39
The Beloved of Whom The Poet Speaks	41
It Isn't, It Is	43
It's A Bird…	45
Fun House	47
What Happens In the Mirror	49
More Visible By Guess	50
Of The Roses, Only Thorns	52
Afterwards	53
I've Been Lost Here Before	55
A Quiet Voice	56
The Kind OF Light	57

I Dreamt I Dwelt in Marble Halls	58
He Departed Before He Arrived	60
My Story	61
Night Heavy With Stars	63
Lock Down 2020	65
Night On Skyline Drive	67
Night Passes	68
Inside Their Veils	69
Breathe Into The Dark	70
The Stars, A Bright Host	71
As The World Woke	72
Moments	73
Not Even The Tip Of A Tail	74
EKG Of A Stunned Heart	76
Invocation To The Angels	78
A Darkness So Massive	81
The Angel of Wrath	83
Quartet	84
There Is No Angel of Music	85
Where He So Intently Stares	87
The Cathedral Fell	88
Scripture	90
The Wild God	91
The Book of The Wild God	93
Secretary to the Stars	94
It Is The Angel	96
The Center Does Not Hold	98
Trail To the River	99
Angel of Lost Bones	101
Spirit Moves	102

Thank you

This has been
A Muddle and A Miracle
by Serena Fusek

In addition to several poetry chapbooks, including two about motorcycling, **Serena Fusek** has three full length collections: **Alphabet of Foxes** (*San Francisco Bay Press*) and **Ancient Maps and a Tarot Pack** *(Bitter Oleander Press), and* **Heartwood Dreams of Blossoms** *(Wider Perspectives Press).*

Garret Hongo calls her a fabulist.

She lives in Virginia with her husband, a varying number of cats, and shelves crammed full of too many books.

colophon
Wider Perspectives Publishing artists published – the list reworked due to the growing library of fine writers coming out of, or even into, the Hampton Roads area of Virginia.

Samantha Casey
Donna Burnett-Robinson
Faith Griffin
Se'Mon-Michelle Rosser
Lisa M. Kendrick
Cassandra IsFree
Nich (Nicholis Williams)
Samantha Geovjian Clarke
Natalie Morison-Uzzle
Gus Woodward II
Patsy Bickerstaff
Edith Blake
Jack Cassada
Dezz
Daniel Garwood
Jada Hollingsworth
Tabetha Moon House
Travis Hailes- Virgo, thePoet
Nick Marickovich
Grey Hues
Rivers Raye
Madeline Garcia
Chichi Iwuorie
Symay Rhodes
Tanya Cunningham
    (Scientific Eve)
Terra Leigh
Raymond M. Simmons
Samantha Borders-Shoemaker
Taz Weysweete'
Ann Shalaski

Jade Leonard
Darean Polk
Bobby K. (The Poor Man's Poet)
J. Scott Wilson (Teech!)
Charles Wilson
Gloria Darlene Mann
Neil Spirtas
Jorge Mendez & JT Williams
Sarah Eileen Williams
Stephanie Diana (Noftz)
Shanya – Lady S.
Jason Brown (Drk Mtr)
Kailyn Rae Sasso
Crickyt J. Expression
Luana Portales
Sonya Fitch
        Crystal Nolen
    Catherine TL Hodges
        Kent Knowlton
        Vanessa Jones
   James Harry Wilson
          Bruce Curb
Willy J. (Jason Williams)

the Hampton Roads Artistic Collective (757 Perspectives) & The Poet's Domain are all WPP literary journals in cooperation with Scientific Eve or Live Wire Press

Check for those artists on FaceBook, Instagram, the Virginia Poetry Online channel on YouTube, and other social media.

www.ingramcontent.com/pod-product-compliance
Lightning Source LLC
Chambersburg PA
CBHW020944090426
42736CB00010B/1263